All New Crafts for Halloween

KATHY ROSS
Illustrated by Sharon Lane Holm

The Millbrook Press • Brookfield, Connecticut

31172052026507

For my sweet little pumpkin, Julianna.
K.R.

For Karen and Sharon,
thanks for always being there.
S.L.H

Library of Congress Cataloging-in-Publication Data
Ross, Kathy (Katharine Reynolds), 1948–
All new crafts for Halloween / Kathy Ross ; illustrated by Sharon Lane Holm.
v. cm. — (All-new holiday crafts for kids)
Contents: Puzzle pieces ghost pin — Can pumpkin favor — Doll clothes scarecrow —
Haunted photograph — Witchy pen — Ghostly tissue box — Jack-o'-lantern antenna
topper — Count Dracula puppet — Batty ear dangles — Floating ghost candy cup —
Changing face magnets — Ghost zipper pull — Peering mummy puppet — Doll masks —
Skeleton scatter pin — Yarn-wrapped black cat — Frankenstein treasure keeper — The
great spider race — Most "eggs"alent Halloween favors — Changing face pumpkin bag —
Safety owl treat bag — Something weird in a jar.
ISBN 0-7613-2554-9 (lib. bdg.) — ISBN 0-7613-1577-2 (pbk.)
1. Halloween decorations—Juvenile literature. 2. Handicraft—Juvenile literature.
[1. Halloween decorations. 2. Handicraft.] I. Holm, Sharon Lane, ill. II. Title. III. Series.
TT900.H32R66 2003   745.594'1646—dc21   2002152688

Published by The Millbrook Press, Inc.
2 Old New Milford Road
Brookfield, Connecticut 06804
www.millbrookpress.com

Printed in the United States of America
5 4 3 2 1 (lib.)
5 4 3 2 1 (pbk.)

Contents

Haunt your collar with this spooky lapel pin.

Puzzle Pieces Ghosts Pin

Here is what you need:

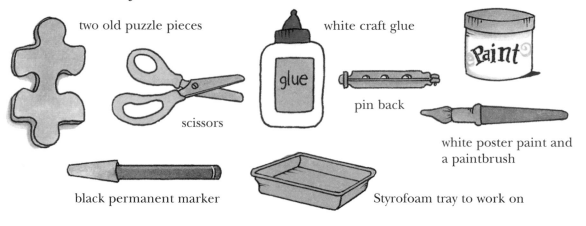

two old puzzle pieces

scissors

white craft glue

glue

pin back

Paint

white poster paint and a paintbrush

black permanent marker

Styrofoam tray to work on

Here is what you do:

1 Choose two puzzle pieces with a round knob on the top and the bottom and two holes on each side. The top pieces that stick out above the hole on each side will become the ghost's arms. Use the scissors to cut away the bottom piece that sticks out under the hole on each side. The pieces should now resemble tiny ghosts.

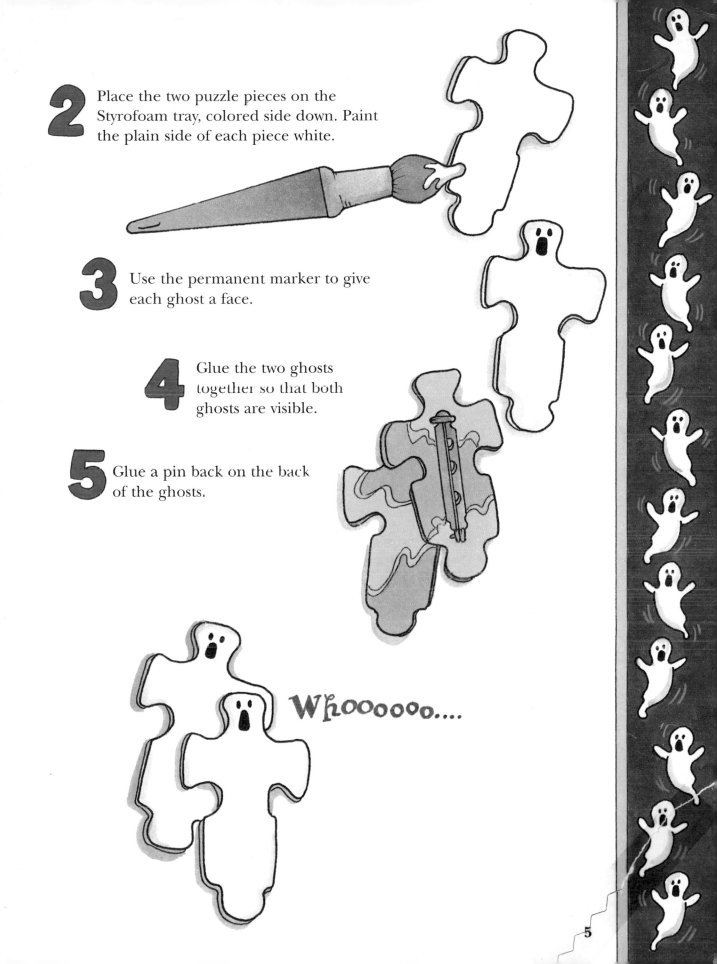

2 Place the two puzzle pieces on the Styrofoam tray, colored side down. Paint the plain side of each piece white.

3 Use the permanent marker to give each ghost a face.

4 Glue the two ghosts together so that both ghosts are visible.

5 Glue a pin back on the back of the ghosts.

Whooooooo....

Turn your Halloween table into a pumpkin patch
with this party favor idea.

Can Pumpkin Favor

Here is what you need:

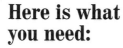

low round can
such as a tuna can

candy and
small toys

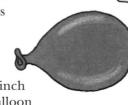

orange 11-inch
(28-cm) balloon

white craft glue

scissors

green
construction
paper

black permanent marker

green pipe cleaner

cardboard paper-towel tube

Here is what you do:

1 Fill the clean, empty can with wrapped candy and small toys.

2 Cut the neck off the orange balloon.

3 Stretch the balloon over the opening of the can and around it to cover the can and make it look like a round orange pumpkin. Be careful not to poke any holes in the balloon with your fingernails!

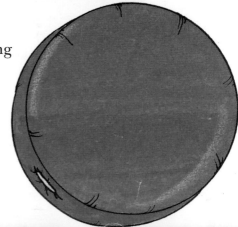

6

4 Use the marker to draw a jack-o'-lantern face on the part of the balloon that is over the opening of the can.

5 Cut a stem for the pumpkin from the green paper. Wrap a piece of green pipe cleaner around your finger to make a vine for the pumpkin. Glue the stem and the vine to the top of the pumpkin.

6 Cut a ¾-inch (2-cm) ring from the cardboard tube for a holder for the pumpkin.

7 Cover the holder with green construction paper. Write the name of the person the pumpkin is for on the holder. Stand the pumpkin on the holder.

Mike

If you have balloons left over from this year's Halloween party, carefully deflate them near the neck and save them to make favors next year. Black balloons would make very nice cat faces.

Mike

Kathy

You will need to borrow some clothes from a doll friend to make this next project.

Doll Clothes Scarecrow

Here is what you need:

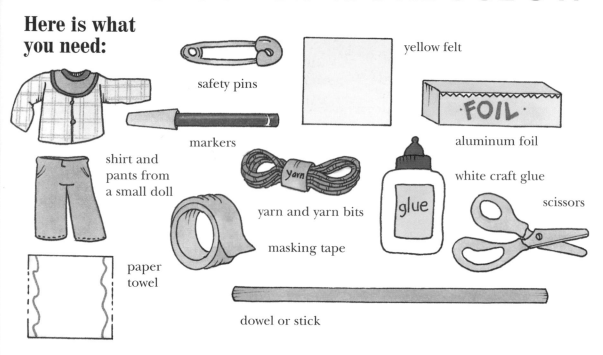

safety pins

yellow felt

markers

aluminum foil

shirt and pants from a small doll

FOIL

yarn and yarn bits

white craft glue

glue

scissors

masking tape

paper towel

dowel or stick

Here is what you do:

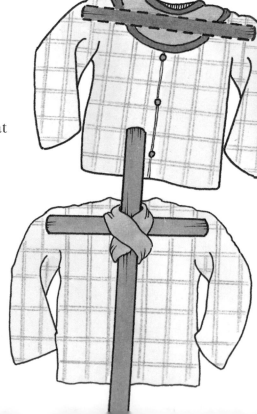

1 Use a safety pin to pin the top of the pants inside the back of the bottom of the shirt.

2 Slip a piece of dowel or stick through the arms of the shirt so that the ends of the two sleeves hang down from the ends of the dowel.

3 Use the masking tape to secure a second dowel to the center of the arm dowel. The dowel needs to be long enough to have an end sticking out at the top so that the head can be secured to the scarecrow and an end

8

sticking out the bottom to use as a stand for the scarecrow. The pants need to be in front of the dowel.

4 Completely close the front of the shirt. Use extra safety pins if needed.

5 Shape a ball of aluminum foil around the top of the dowel for the head. Use yarn to tie a square of paper towel over the foil head. Use the markers to give the scarecrow a face.

6 Cut the front and back of a hat for the scarecrow from the felt. Glue yarn bits around the inside brim of the hat so that the yarn hangs down to look like hair.

7 Glue the front and the back of the hat together over the top of the head of the scarecrow. Tie a piece of yarn around the hat to decorate it.

8 Stuff yarn pieces into the ends of the shirt and pants so that they stick out to look like straw.

Maybe a grown-up in your house would like to have the scarecrow stand guard in a houseplant this fall.

Even your pen can have a disguise for Halloween!

Witchy Pen

Here is what you need:

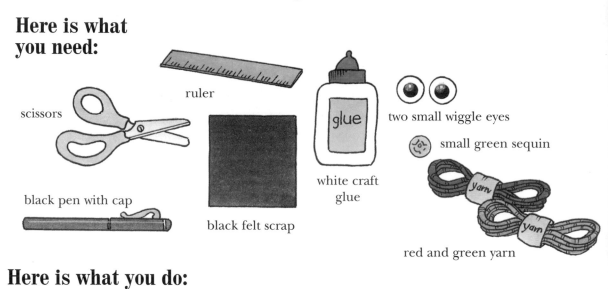

ruler

scissors

two small wiggle eyes

small green sequin

glue

white craft glue

black pen with cap

black felt scrap

red and green yarn

Here is what you do:

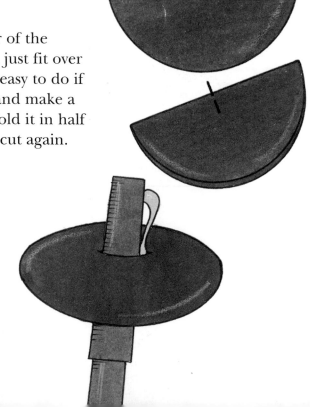

1 Cut a 2-inch (5-cm) circle of black felt to make the brim of the hat.

2 Cut a small X in the center of the circle so that the circle will just fit over the cap of the pen. This is easy to do if you fold the circle in half and make a tiny cut on the fold, then fold it in half in the other direction and cut again.

3 Slide the circle halfway down the cap of the pen so that half the cap forms the top part of the hat above the brim.

4 The face of the witch will be on the opposite side from the pen clip if there is one. Glue the two wiggle eyes on the face area below the hat brim. Glue the green sequin below the eyes for a nose.

5 Cut a tiny piece of red yarn. Unravel one strand from the yarn. Glue the strand below the nose for a mouth.

6 Cut several 2-inch (5-cm) pieces of green yarn. Glue the yarn around the brim of the hat on each side and behind the face for the hair.

These would make great party favors, but don't let the "witch" turn all your guests into toads!

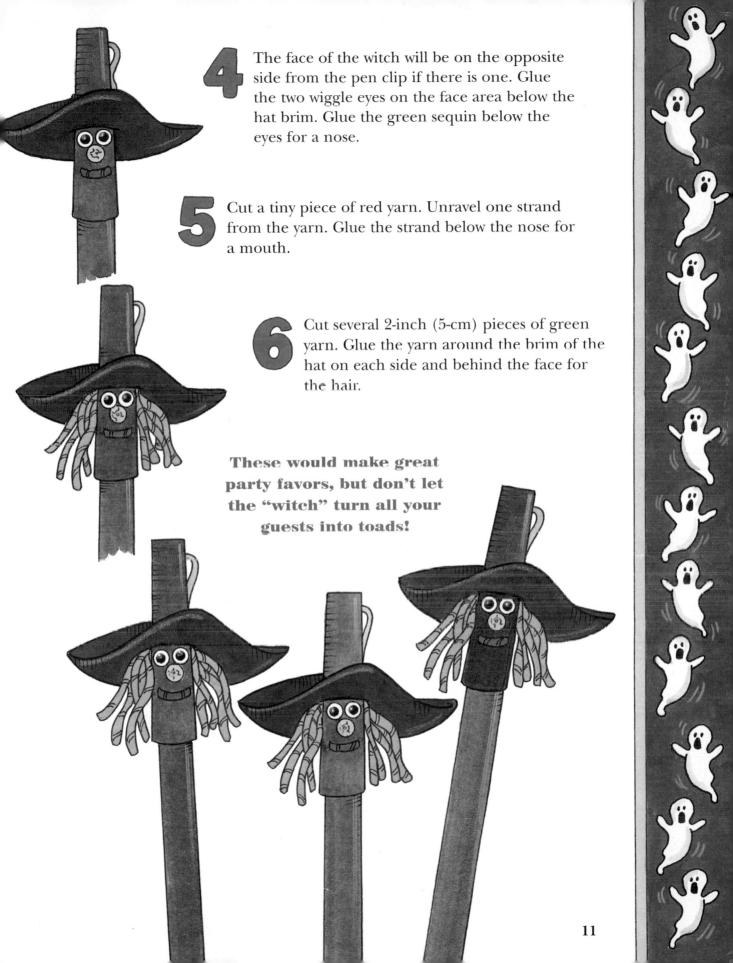

Get your car ready for Halloween.

Jack-o'-Lantern Antenna Marker

Here is what you need:

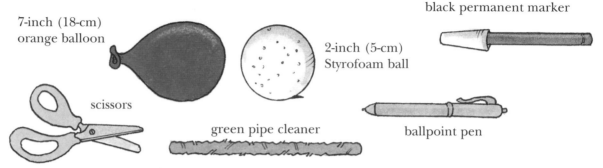

black permanent marker

7-inch (18-cm)
orange balloon

2-inch (5-cm)
Styrofoam ball

scissors

green pipe cleaner

ballpoint pen

Here is what you do:

1 Cut the neck off the orange balloon.

2 Stretch the balloon over the Styrofoam ball to cover it.

3 Use the black marker to draw a jack-o'-lantern face on the balloon-covered ball above the opening of the balloon, which will be the bottom of the pumpkin.

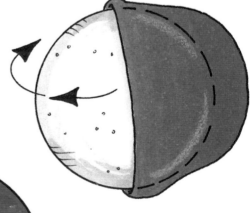

12

4 Cut a ½-inch (1.25-cm) piece of green pipe cleaner. Push the pipe cleaner into the top of the pumpkin for a stem, being careful not to puncture the balloon, but rather pushing the balloon down into the Styrofoam with the stem. If you do this step carefully the balloon won't rip.

5 Use the ballpoint pen to poke a small hole in the bottom of the pumpkin. This will make it easy to slip the ball over the tip of the car antenna.

Not only will this antenna decoration make your car look decorated for Halloween, it will also make the car easy to spot in a crowded parking lot.

Watch out for this guy when he opens his mouth!

Count Dracula Puppet

Here is what you need:

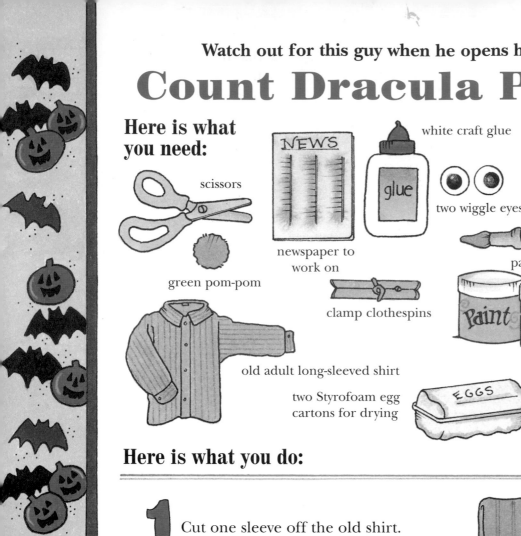

scissors

green pom-pom

NEWS

newspaper to work on

clamp clothespins

white craft glue

glue

two wiggle eyes

paintbrush

Paint Paint

green and black paint

tennis ball

two white twist ties

black and red permanent marker

old adult long-sleeved shirt

two Styrofoam egg cartons for drying

EGGS

Here is what you do:

1 Cut one sleeve off the old shirt. This will be the body of the puppet.

2 Paint the entire sleeve black and let it dry overnight on the Styrofoam egg carton.

3 When the sleeve dries it will be stiff from the paint. Fold the excess sleeve at the opening up inside itself so that the sleeve body is about 9 inches (23 cm) tall. This should give the body enough strength to stand without further support.

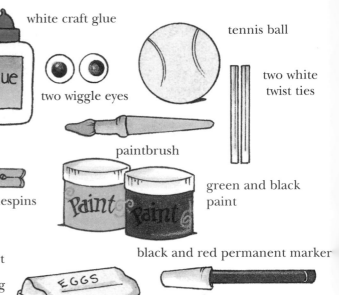

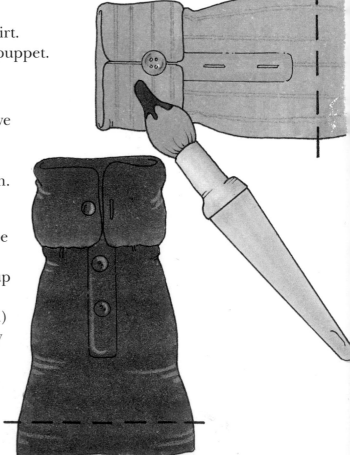

4 Ask an adult to use a serrated knife to cut a slit across the bottom half of the tennis ball for the mouth of the puppet.

5 Paint the tennis ball green and let it dry on the Styrofoam egg carton.

6 Squeeze the cut mouth of the tennis ball on both sides to open it. Color the top and bottom of the mouth with red marker.

7 Use the black marker to color hair on the puppet.

8 Glue on the two wiggle eyes and the green pom-pom for a nose.

9 Fold the two twist ties in half at a slight angle so that the fold forms a pointed tooth. Glue the ends of each twist tie up inside the mouth so that a tooth hangs down on each side. Do not try to fold the two teeth down and arrange them until the glue has dried.

10 Glue the head of the puppet inside the cuff of the body. Fold the two sides of the cuff down and glue the rest of the opening shut. If you need to, hold the glued parts together with clamp clothespins until the glue has completely dried.

To use the puppet, stand it on one hand and squeeze each side of the mouth with the other.

Weird!

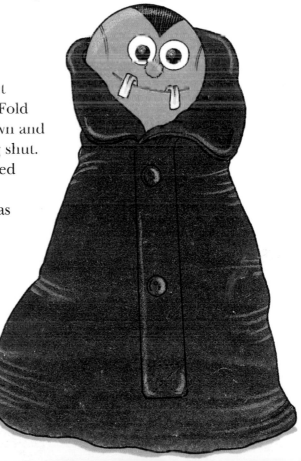

Make some bats to hang around you!

Batty Ear Dangles

Here is what you need:

black yarn

ruler

four tiny wiggle eyes

scissors

white craft glue

black permanent marker

two uncooked shell macaroni

black felt scraps

Here is what you do:

1 Cut two 6- to 7-inch (15- to 18-cm) lengths of black yarn, enough to loop over your ear and hang down 1 inch (2.5 cm) or so.

6"

2 Glue the ends of each piece of yarn inside one of the shell macaroni. Hang the yarn over your ear. If the shell hangs down too low, glue more of the yarn inside the shell, until the shell hangs just below your ear.

16

3 If the shell macaronis are not completely filled with black yarn, glue in more yarn bits to fill.

4 Use the permanent marker to color the outside of the shells black.

5 Fold the black felt in half and cut a black bat wing for each shell. Open each wing so that there are two wings for each shell. Wrap felt bat wings around the back and sides of each shell. If you want your bats hanging upside down be sure to put the wings on upside down, too.

6 Glue two tiny wiggle eyes to the yarn-filled part of the bats.

When the glue has completely dried, the bats will be ready to hang from your ears! Shhh . . . do you hear a

Whoosh?

17

Amaze your guests with this spooky candy cup idea.

Floating Ghost Candy Cup

Here is what you need:

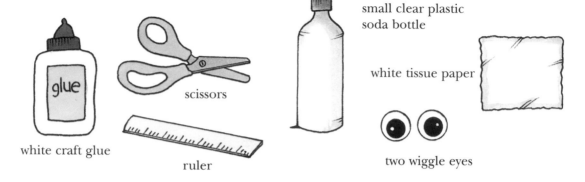

glue

white craft glue

scissors

ruler

small clear plastic soda bottle

white tissue paper

two wiggle eyes

Here is what you do:

1 Cut off the top half of the bottle so that the bottom is about 4 inches (10 cm) tall.

2 Cut a 1-inch (2.5-cm)-wide spiral band around the rim, going around only once. The band should still be attached to the bottle bottom, which will be the candy container.

3 Round off the cut end of the band. Pull the band up and away from the bottle bottom.

4 Cut a 6-inch (15-cm) square of white tissue paper.

5 Glue the tissue paper over the rounded end of the band to look like a ghost floating above the candy container.

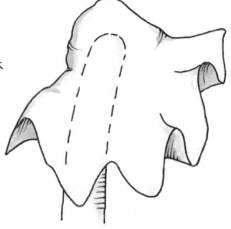

6 Glue the two wiggle eyes on the head of the ghost.

Fill the candy container with Halloween goodies.

Yum Yum!

Changing Face Magnets

Here is what you need:

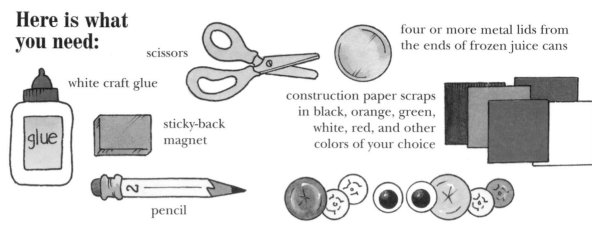

scissors

white craft glue

sticky-back magnet

glue

pencil

four or more metal lids from the ends of frozen juice cans

construction paper scraps in black, orange, green, white, red, and other colors of your choice

collage items such as craft gems, sequins, and wiggle eyes

Here is what you do:

1 Cover one side of one of the metal lids with orange construction paper. To do this use the pencil to trace around the lid on the paper, cut the circle out, and glue it over one side of the lid. Cover a second lid with black paper and a third lid with green paper.

2 Cut black shapes for the orange-covered lid to make several different jack-o'-lantern faces. You can make some triangle-shaped pieces for the eyes and nose, some round ones, etc. You can also cut happy, sad, and scary-looking mouths for the pumpkin. Cut a stem from the green paper and also one or more silly hats for the pumpkin.

3 Put a piece of sticky-back magnet on the back of each piece you have made for the pumpkin so that the pieces will stick to the metal lid. You might also want to use some collage items to make pumpkin faces such as wiggle eyes, sequins, and craft gems. Just add a piece of sticky-back magnet to any items you want to include.

4 For the black lid cut features to make cat faces and wings, teeth, and eyes for a bat. You can also use some of the items you have already made for the jack-o'-lantern magnet. Add a piece of sticky-back magnet to each new piece.

5 For the green lid cut monster features. You can use lots of the pieces you have already made, but you might want to add some different teeth, a big red mouth, and some large ears.

6 Put a strip of sticky-back magnet on the backs of all four lids. The last lid can be used to store the extra pieces. If you have made lots of features you may even need two storage lids.

Hang the magnets on the refrigerator. These changing faces will have your friends and family wondering.

Give your jacket or backpack a Halloween look with this idea.

Ghost Zipper Pull

Here is what you need:

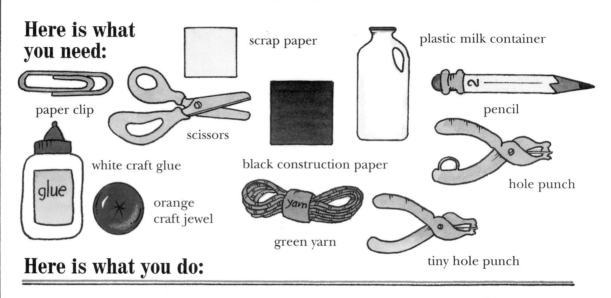

paper clip

scissors

scrap paper

plastic milk container

pencil

white craft glue

black construction paper

hole punch

glue

orange
craft jewel

green yarn

tiny hole punch

Here is what you do:

1 Draw a small ghost shape on the scrap paper. When you get a shape you like, cut the shape out to use as a pattern.

2 Cut one side from the plastic milk container. Draw around the pattern on the piece of plastic.

3 Cut the ghost shape out.

4 Use the regular hole punch to punch two eyes and a nose in the head of the ghost.

5 Glue the orange craft jewel on one side of the ghost to look like the ghost is carrying it. If you do not have a craft jewel cut a pumpkin from orange felt or paper.

6 Cut tiny features for the pumpkin from the black construction paper. Glue the features to the craft jewel to make it look like a jack-o'-lantern.

7 Cut tiny pieces of yarn for the stem. If the yarn is too thick, unravel a thread from the yarn to use. Glue the yarn stem to the top of the jack-o'-lantern.

8 Use the tiny hole punch to make a hole at the top of the ghost. Slip a paper clip through the hole to hang the ghost. Attach the ghost to the zipper pull on your jacket or backpack.

You might want to make a different Halloween zipper pull. Maybe a jack-o'-lantern cut from an orange plastic bottle or a monster cut from a green one.

Ooooo!

Peering Mummy Puppet

Here is what you need:

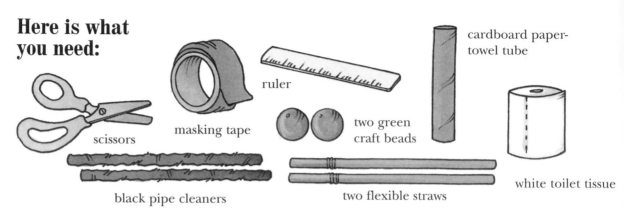

scissors

masking tape

ruler

two green craft beads

cardboard paper-towel tube

white toilet tissue

black pipe cleaners

two flexible straws

Here is what you do:

1 Cut the end off the cardboard tube so that it is about 9 inches (23 cm) tall.

2 Cut a 1 by 2-inch (2.5 by 5 cm) eye opening out of one end.

3 Wrap the tube with toilet tissue to look like a mummy without covering the eye opening. Use masking tape to secure the ends of the toilet tissue inside the top and the bottom of the tube.

4 Cut two 3-inch (8-cm) pieces of black pipe cleaner. Slide a green craft bead on the end of each piece and bend the end down to secure the beads.

5 Put the end of each pipe cleaner down in the flexible end of a straw so that the bead rests on the top opening of the straw.

6 Tape the two straws together, side by side, and bend the eyes slightly away from each other.

7 Put the eyes up inside the mummy so that they are visible through the eye opening.

To use the puppet hold the mummy in one hand and the bottom of the straws in the other. Practice making the eyes appear to look around then disappear back into the wrappings.

Creepy!

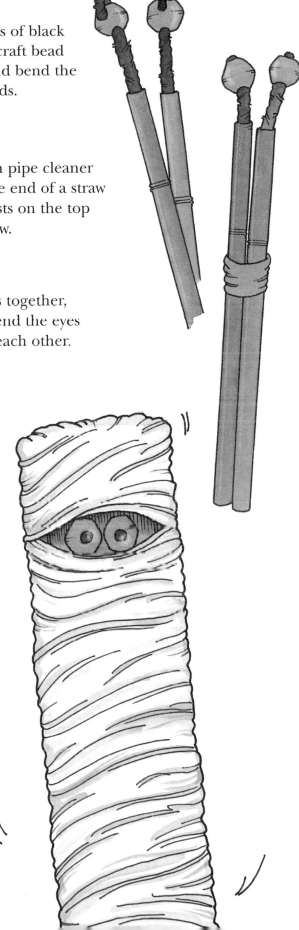

Even your doll friends can have a Halloween disguise!

Doll Masks

Here is what you need:

scissors

white craft glue

aluminum foil

catalogs or magazines
with Halloween items

ballpoint pen

small hole punch

elastic thread

Here is what you do:

1 Find a Halloween face in a magazine or catalog that is slightly larger than the face of the doll you are making the mask for. Cut the magazine face out.

2 Cut a square of aluminum foil that is twice as wide as the magazine face.

3 Glue the magazine face to the center of the aluminum foil square.

4 While the glue is wet, shape the magazine face part of the foil over the face of your doll. The excess foil will prevent any glue from getting on the doll. Gently press the mask around the nose and mouth of the doll and into the eye sockets. This will give the mask a shape.

5 When the glue has dried completely, carefully cut away the excess aluminum foil around the edges.

6 Use the ballpoint pen to carefully punch eyeholes in the mask where the mask dips in for the eye sockets on the doll. Just like with a real mask, the eyeholes may not be where the eyes on the mask appear.

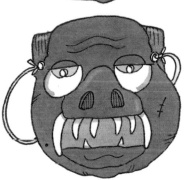

7 Use the small hole punch to make a hole in each side of the mask. Cut a piece of elastic thread. Tic an end through one side of the mask. Use the head of the doll to measure how long the elastic will need to be. Tic the other end of the elastic to the other side of the mask and trim off any excess elastic thread.

All your dolls will probably want a mask.

This scatter pin looks great pinned on clothes or a curtain.

Skeleton Scatter Pin

Here is what you need:

white cotton swabs

scissors

black permanent marker

white craft glue

thin orange and/or black ribbon or yarn

two pin backs

dried lima beans

Styrofoam tray to work on

Here is what you do:

1 Cut a 1-inch (2.5-cm) piece of stick from the middle part of a cotton swab for the body of the person skeleton.

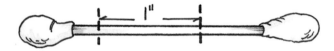

2 Use the black marker to draw a face on one of the lima beans to make a head for the skeleton. Working on the Styrofoam tray, glue the head to the top of the stick body.

3 Cut a swab in half for the legs and feet. Glue the tops of the legs to the bottom of the stick body.

4 Cut arms for the skeleton from the two opposite ends of a swab. Glue the arms in place on the top portion of the stick body.

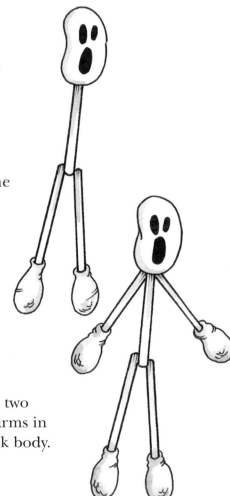

28

5 Cut three ribs for the skeleton from the stick of a cotton swab. Glue the ribs across the stick body of the skeleton.

6 To make the dog skeleton cut a piece of stick from the center of a swab for the body.

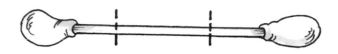

7 Use the black marker to draw a face on a lima bean for the head. Glue the head to one end of the stick body, again working on the Styrofoam tray.

8 Cut four legs for the dog from the ends of cotton swabs. Glue the legs coming down from the body.

9 Cut a piece of stick from a cotton swab to make a tail for the dog. Glue the tail to the end of the body, sticking up.

10 Cut a piece of ribbon or yarn for each skeleton. Tie each piece in a knot at the center, then trim the ends to make bow ties. Glue a bow tie at the neck of each skeleton. Let the skeletons dry overnight.

11 When the skeletons are dry, peel them off the Styrofoam tray. Cut a piece of yarn or ribbon for a leash. Tie one end around the hand of the skeleton and the other around the neck of the dog skeleton. The leash should end up being about 2 inches (5 cm) long.

12 Glue a pin back to the back of each skeleton.

If you want to make the skeletons to play with rather than to wear, just add a piece of sticky-back magnet to the back of each one and stick them on the refrigerator.

Even a box of tissues can become a Halloween decoration!

Ghostly Tissue Box

Here is what you need:

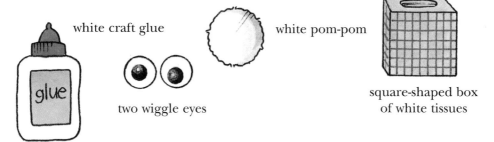

white craft glue

two wiggle eyes

white pom-pom

square-shaped box
of white tissues

Here is what you do:

1 Turn the tissue box on one side so that the tissue hangs down.

2 Glue two wiggle eyes on the clear plastic over the opening above the tissue.

3 Glue the white pom-pom below the eyes for a nose.

Each time a tissue "ghost" is pulled out, a new one will appear until the box is empty.

Yarn-Wrapped Black Cat

Here is what you need:

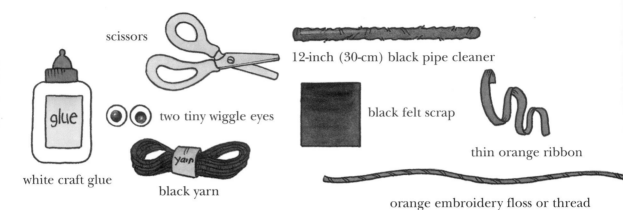

scissors

12-inch (30-cm) black pipe cleaner

glue

two tiny wiggle eyes

black felt scrap

thin orange ribbon

white craft glue

black yarn

orange embroidery floss or thread

Here is what you do:

1 Cut the black pipe cleaner in half. One of the pieces will form the frame for the body, head, and tail of the cat.

2 Cut the second piece in half to use for the legs of the cat. Wrap one piece around the body about 2 inches (5 cm) from the end for the front legs and the other piece about 2 inches (5 cm) from the opposite end for the back legs.

3 Fold one end of the body piece in half for the head. Bend up the other end of the body piece for the tail.

4 Unravel a very long piece of yarn. If you run out before the cat is completely wrapped in yarn you can cut another piece.

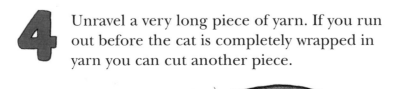

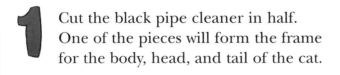

5 Start wrapping the frame of the cat in yarn. You can secure the end by holding it against one of the pipe cleaner legs and wrapping the yarn around it. As you finish wrapping the legs and tail, bend up the ends of the pipe cleaners to keep the yarn from slipping off. You can make different parts of the body thicker by wrapping more layers of yarn. You will want the tail and legs to be quite thin, but the body should be thicker and the head should be wrapped until it becomes a round ball of yarn.

6 When you are done wrapping the frame, tie off the end of the yarn and cut off any excess yarn.

7 Cut tiny triangle-shaped ears for the cat from the black felt. Glue the ears to the top of the head. Glue the wiggle eyes on the head of the cat below the ears.

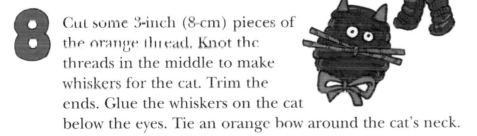

8 Cut some 3-inch (8-cm) pieces of the orange thread. Knot the threads in the middle to make whiskers for the cat. Trim the ends. Glue the whiskers on the cat below the eyes. Tie an orange bow around the cat's neck.

9 Dip the tips of the tail and feet and the top of the head in glue to secure the yarn and keep it from slipping off the frame.

When the glue has dried, you will be able to pose the cat by carefully bending the pipe-cleaner frame.

Make a monster to hide your very important stuff!

Frankenstein Treasure Keeper

Here is what you need:

scissors

short plastic detergent bottle

aluminum foil

FOIL

glue

white craft glue

thin red ribbon

black and white construction paper scraps

ruler

old black sock

two paper fasteners

black permanent marker

plastic cap from salad dressing or spice jar

Here is what you do:

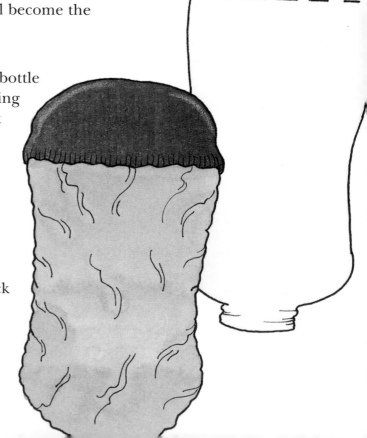

1 Cut off the bottom of the plastic bottle. The open bottom of the bottle will become the top of the head.

2 Cover the outside of the bottle with aluminum foil, tucking the ends inside the spout to close it. Fold the ends down into the cutout bottom of the bottle so that the opening is not covered up.

3 Cut a 3-inch (8-cm) piece from the toe end of the black sock. Pull the piece down over the opening to hide it and to become the hair for the monster.

34

4 Cut eyes from the black and white paper scraps. Glue the eyes to the front of the bottle.

5 Cut a strip of red ribbon for the mouth. Glue the mouth to the face of the monster. Use the black marker to draw a nose on the face.

6 Cut a small slit in the foil just below the hair on each side of the face. Bend the end of one of the paper fasteners. Dip the bent end in glue and slide it under the foil through the cut slit so that the paper fastener sticks out on the side of the head to look like a screw. Do the same thing with the second paper fastener on the opposite side of the head.

7 Use the black marker to write "Keep Away" or some other warning on the side of the plastic cap. Glue the spout of the bottle inside the cap so that the monster will stand.

Remove the sock hair to hide things in the head of the monster. Cover the opening again with the sock and no one will know your secret.

Ughh!

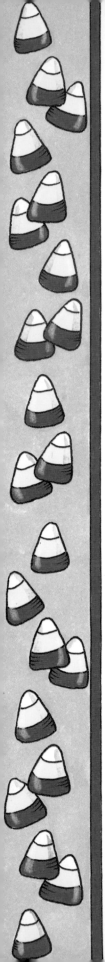

Get together with a friend for . . .

The Great Spider Race

Here is what you need:

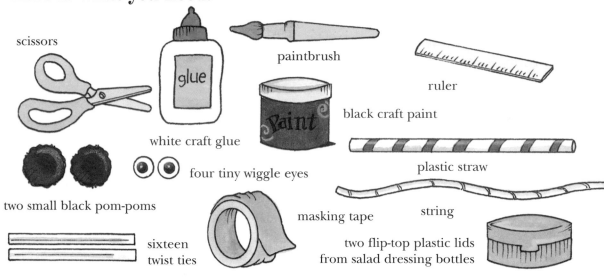

scissors

white craft glue

paintbrush

ruler

black craft paint

plastic straw

four tiny wiggle eyes

two small black pom-poms

masking tape

string

sixteen twist ties

two flip-top plastic lids from salad dressing bottles

Here is what you do:

1 To make each spider, open a lid and place the ends of eight twist ties in the cap so that they stick out on each side to form the legs of the spider. Glue them in place and secure them with masking tape. Close the lid.

2 Bend each leg in the middle to form knees. Bend the ends out to form feet.

3 Glue a black pom-pom between the legs on one side of the cap for the head. Glue two wiggle eyes on the head.

4 Cut a 1-inch (2.5-cm) piece of plastic straw. Glue the piece of straw to the back of the spider. Secure the straw with masking tape. Let the glue dry completely.

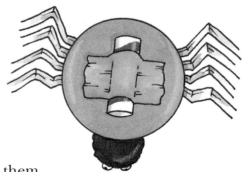

5 You can paint the spiders black or leave them the colors of the materials you made them from.

6 To race the spiders, cut two 10-foot (3-m) lengths of string. Tie one end of each string to the bottom of a chair leg. Slide a spider onto the other end of each string through the straw on the back. At the signal to start, both spiders can be released to slide down the string. The first spider to reach the end is the winner.

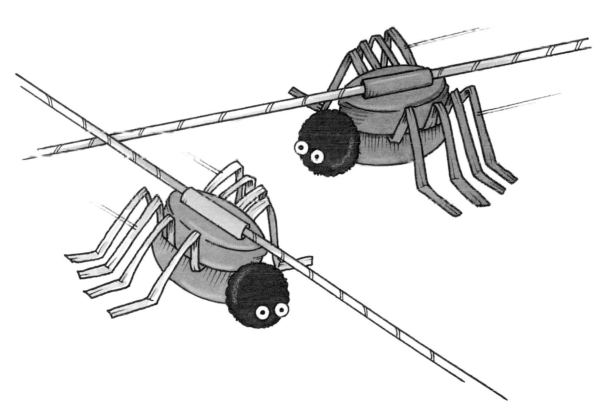

You can have spider races alone or with friends. Additional lines can be added to include more spiders in the race.

These Halloween party favors are "eggs"tra special.

Most "Eggs"ellent Halloween Favors

Here is what you need:

scissors

white craft glue

glue

green pipe cleaner

black felt scraps

Paint

orange poster paint and a paintbrush

masking tape

black permanent marker

Halloween candy and small prizes

empty, cleaned eggshells that have been cracked at one end

eggs

Styrofoam egg carton for drying

plastic soda bottle twist caps

Here is what you do:

1 Next time your family has eggs ask the person making the eggs to carefully crack them on one end to empty the contents from the shell. The eggshells should then be washed and placed, hole down, on the Styrofoam egg carton to dry. You will need an eggshell for each favor you want to make.

2 Fill the empty shell through the opening with wrapped Halloween candy and small prizes. Cover the opening with small strips of masking tape.

3 To make a ghost, turn the filled shell so that the tape is on the bottom. Use the black marker to give the shell a ghost face. You might want to draw arms, too.

4 Glue the bottom of the ghost to the open side of a plastic cap to make it stand. Use the marker to write the name of the person the favor is for across the front of the cap.

5 To make a pumpkin, paint the eggshell orange and let it dry on the Styrofoam egg carton.

6 Fill the eggshell with Halloween candy and prizes and cover the opening with small strips of masking tape.

7 Use the marker to draw a jack-o'-lantern face on the orange shell or cut a face from the black felt scraps and glue it on.

8 Cut a piece of green pipe cleaner for a stem. Glue the stem to the top of the pumpkin.

9 Glue the bottom of the pumpkin to the open side of a plastic bottle cap to make it stand.

10 Use the marker to write the name of the person the favor is for across the front of the cap.

Kathy

Gracie

Mike

Heather

Can you think of some other Halloween characters to make from eggshells? How about a bat or a green monster?

39

Haunted Photograph

Here is what you need:

paintbrush

glow-in-the-dark paints   plastic wrap   photograph framed
under glass

Here is what you do:

1 Select a photograph with one or more people in it. Think
about the placement and size of each spooky character you are
going to make to add to the photograph.

2 Spread a piece of plastic wrap out on a flat surface where
it will be undisturbed overnight.

40

3 Use the glow-in-the-dark paints to draw spooky characters and eyes on the plastic wrap. Fill the drawings in with the paint so that each drawing is solid.

4 When the paint has dried completely overnight, the characters will be ready to be removed from the plastic wrap. Carefully peel each character off the plastic wrap and stick it to the glass over the photograph. The dried paint will stick to the glass but peel off easily after Halloween.

Spooky! And even spookier in the dark!

This trick or treat bag can be used as a game until the big night.

Changing Face Pumpkin Bag

Here is what you need:

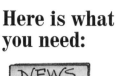
newspaper to work on

9-inch (23-cm) uncoated paper plate

cellophane tape

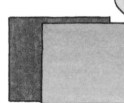
paintbrush

black and green construction paper

scissors

orange poster paint

five paper fasteners

old gift bag, plain if possible

Here is what you do:

1 Paint the eating side of the paper plate orange for the pumpkin. Let the paint dry.

2 Put paper fasteners through the plate at the places where the eyes, the nose, and the mouth will be. Do not fold the fasteners tight to the plate, but rather put them about halfway through the plate and spread the sides to secure them. They will act as "buttons" to attach the face pieces.

3 Cut lots of different-shaped face pieces for the pumpkin from the black paper.

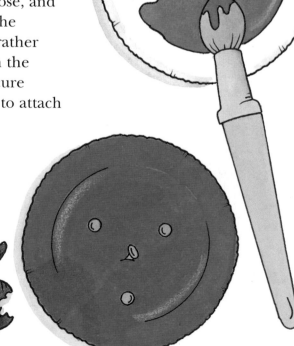

4 Cover one side of each piece with a strip of cellophane tape.

5 Bend each piece in half without creasing it and cut a small slit in the middle, through the tape, to act as the "buttonhole" for attaching each piece to the pumpkin.

6 Cut a stem for the pumpkin from the green construction paper. Cut one or more funny hats for the pumpkin.

7 Cover the back of each new piece with a strip of cellophane tape and fold it to cut the "buttonhole" slit.

8 Poke a paper fastener through the top of the pumpkin where the stem will go. Use the fastener to attach the top of the pumpkin to the top of the bag. Again, you should only put the fastener about halfway through before folding the sides to secure the pumpkin to the bag. This fastener will be the button for the stem and funny hats you make for the pumpkin.

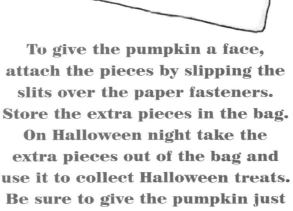

To give the pumpkin a face, attach the pieces by slipping the slits over the paper fasteners. Store the extra pieces in the bag. On Halloween night take the extra pieces out of the bag and use it to collect Halloween treats. Be sure to give the pumpkin just the right face for the big night!

Happy Halloween!

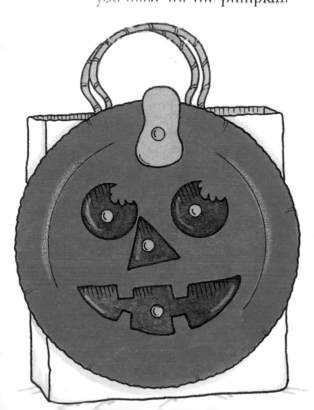

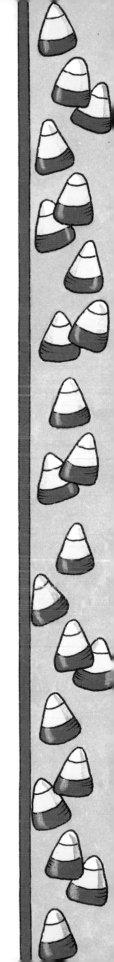

43

Reflecting eyes make this Halloween owl a wise choice for a treat bag.

Safety Owl Treat Bag

Here is what you need:

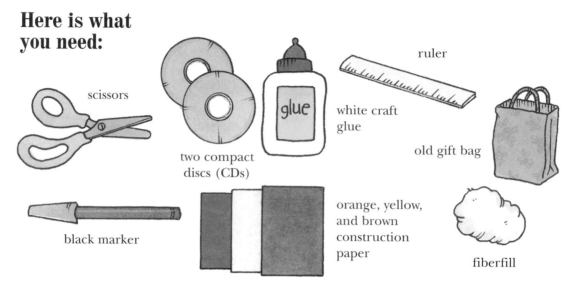

scissors

two compact discs (CDs)

glue

white craft glue

ruler

old gift bag

black marker

orange, yellow, and brown construction paper

fiberfill

Here is what you do:

1 To make the eyes for the owl, cut two 2-inch (5-cm) squares of yellow paper. Glue a square of the yellow paper on the print side, over the hole, of each of the CDs.

2 Turn each CD over so that the shiny side is the front of each eye. Use the marker to color the paper in the center of each eye black for the pupils.

3 Glue the eyes, overlapping at the center if necessary, to the top of one side of the gift bag.

4 Cut a triangle beak for the owl from the orange paper. Slide the end of the beak into the glue under the center part of the eyes.

5 Cut two feet for the owl from the orange paper. Glue the feet to the bottom of the bag.

6 Cover the remainder of the side of the bag with a thin layer of fiberfill "feathers."

7 Cut two long strips of brown paper for the wings. Fold the strips back and forth, accordion-style, like a fan.

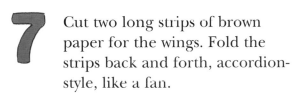

8 Glue the end of a wing to the fold in each side of the bag.

The large reflecting eyes on the owl will reflect the light from car headlights, making you very easy to see.

Something Weird in a Jar

Here is what you need:

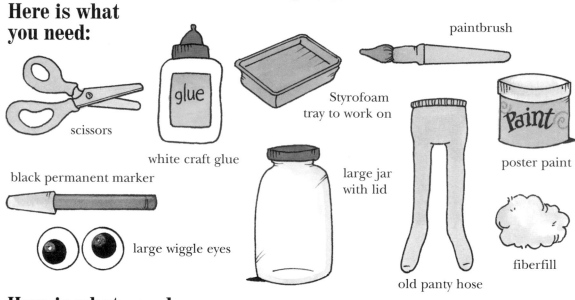

scissors

white craft glue

Styrofoam tray to work on

paintbrush

poster paint

black permanent marker

large wiggle eyes

large jar with lid

old panty hose

fiberfill

Here is what you do:

1 Cut a foot off the old panty hose to use for the weird thing.

2 Stuff the foot with fiberfill, making sure it is not too big to fit inside the jar.

3 Knot the end of the stuffed stocking to close it, then trim off any excess panty hose.

4 Working on the Styrofoam tray, paint the entire weird thing one or more weird colors. Let the thing dry completely on the Styrofoam tray.

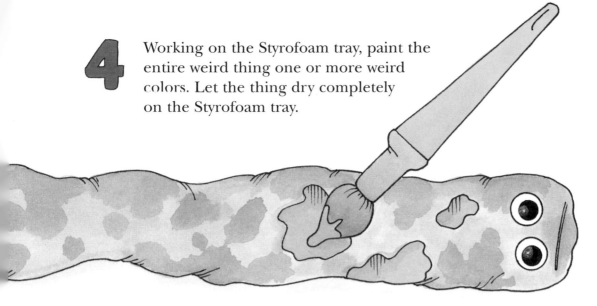

5 Glue the two wiggle eyes to the toe end of the weird thing. Let the glue dry before continuing.

6 Stuff the weird thing into the jar and put the lid on.

7 Use the black marker to write a warning on the jar lid in case someone is thinking of opening it.

Open the jar at your own risk!

Yuk!

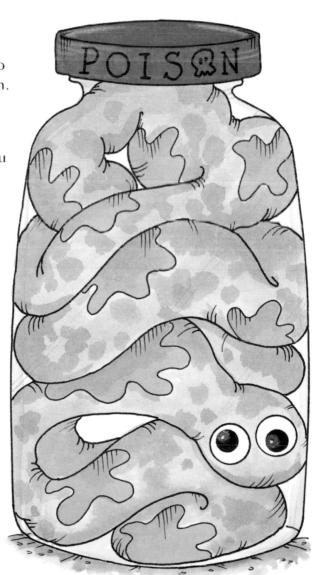

About the Author and Artist

Thirty years as a teacher and director of nursery school programs have given Kathy Ross extensive experience in guiding young children through craft projects. Among the more than forty craft books she has written are *Crafts for All Seasons, Make Yourself a Monster, Crafts From Your Favorite Children's Songs, Kathy Ross Crafts Letter Shapes,* and *Star-Spangled Crafts.* To find out more about Kathy, visit her Web site: *www.Kathyross.com.*

Sharon Lane Holm, a resident of New Fairfield, Connecticut, won awards for her work in advertising design before shifting her concentration to children's books. Her recent books include *Sidewalk Games Around the World, Happy Birthday, Everywhere!, Happy New Year, Everywhere!,* and *Merry Christmas, Everywhere!,* all by Arlene Erlbach; and *Beautiful Bats* by Linda Glaser.

Together, Kathy Ross and Sharon Lane Holm have also created *The Best Christmas Crafts Ever!,* as well as the popular Holiday Crafts for Kids series and the Crafts for Kids Who Are Wild About series.